D1191688

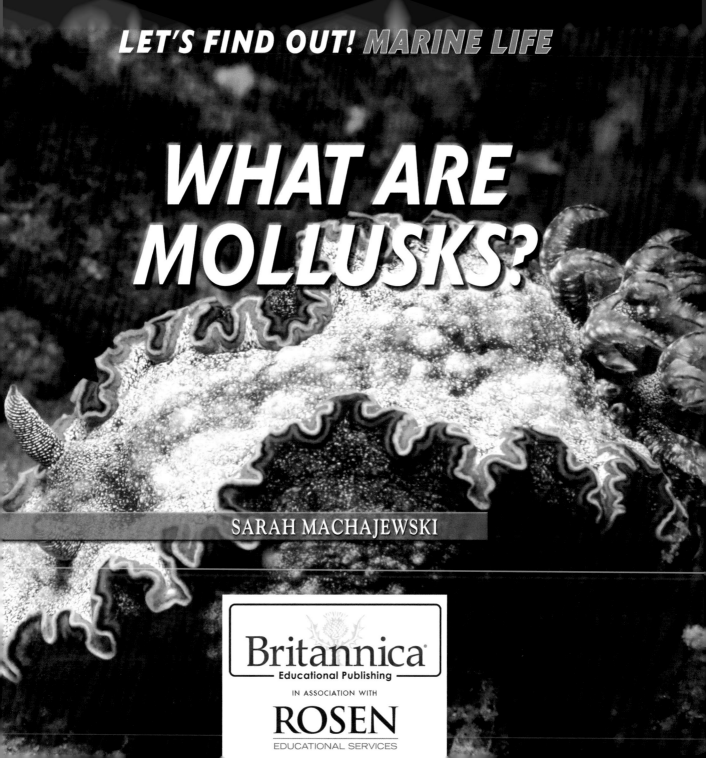

WHAT ARE MOLLUSKS?

SARAH MACHAJEWSKI

Britannica®
Educational Publishing

IN ASSOCIATION WITH

ROSEN
EDUCATIONAL SERVICES

Published in 2017 by Britannica Educational Publishing (a trademark of Encyclopædia Britannica, Inc.) in association with The Rosen Publishing Group, Inc.
29 East 21st Street, New York, NY 10010

Distributed exclusively by Rosen Publishing.
To see additional Britannica Educational Publishing titles, go to rosenpublishing.com.

First Edition

Library of Congress Cataloging-in-Publication Data

Names: Machajewski, Sarah, author.
Title: What are mollusks? / Sarah Machajewski.
Description: First edition. | New York : Britannica Educational Publishing in association with Rosen Educational Services, 2017. | Series: Let's find out! Marine life | Includes bibliographical references and index.
Identifiers: LCCN 2016020466| ISBN 9781508103875 (library bound) | ISBN 9781508103882 (pbk.) | ISBN 9781508103141 (6-pack).
Subjects: LCSH: Mollusks—Juvenile literature. | Aquatic animals—Juvenile literature.
Classification: LCC QL405.2 .M34 2017 | DDC 594—dc23
LC record available at https://lccn.loc.gov/2016020466

Manufactured in China

CONTENTS

Meet the Mollusks

This coconut octopus is just one of the many mollusks that call Earth home.

Our planet is home to millions of creatures. From sea turtles to snakes to snow leopards, Earth's **habitats** are filled with animals that are interesting and diverse, including mollusks! There are many fascinating animals within the group of mollusks. Mollusks share many things in

VOCABULARY

Habitats are places or type of places where a plant or animal naturally lives or grows.

common, yet there are also many differences between them. Most mollusks live in water, though some live on land. Many mollusks have shells, but some do not. In fact, some mollusks, such as snails and squid, seem too different to belong to the same group.

Millions of mollusks populate our planet. They live in diverse environments all over the world. Mollusks have certain characteristics that set them apart from other animals—and each other. Let's dive into the world of mollusks to learn more about them.

Mollusks live in many different environments, including rivers.

Identifying Mollusks

A mollusk is a kind of animal with a soft body. Most mollusks have a hard shell that protects their body, but not all do. There are more than 100,000 species, or kinds, of mollusks in the world. Scientists think they account for 23 percent of all known sea animals.

With so many mollusk species, it's no surprise how different they are. But they do have some traits in

This Carpathian blue slug creeps along a pile of moss.

THINK ABOUT IT

Why do mollusks need to have a hard shell? What could happen without it?

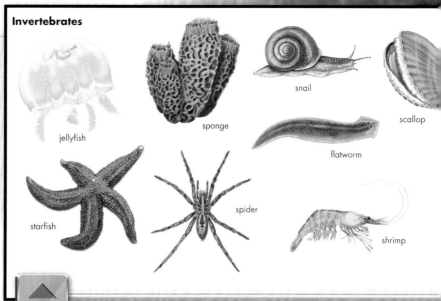

Invertebrates

jellyfish
sponge
snail
scallop
flatworm
starfish
spider
shrimp

More than 90 percent of all animals are invertebrates, including jellyfish, starfish, snails, shrimp, and more!

common. Mollusks are invertebrates, which means they do not have a backbone, and their bodies are not divided into sections. Generally, mollusks have three body regions—a head, a visceral mass, and a foot-like structure. The head contains the brain. The visceral mass contains the organs. It is surrounded by a protective layer called the mantle. In some mollusks, the mantle forms the animal's shell. A mollusk's "foot" helps it move or dig.

Mollusks are divided into seven classes based on shared traits. Even then, mollusks in the same class are varied. They can be different sizes and colors, behave differently, and live in different habitats.

The bivalves include oysters, clams, and mussels. These mollusks have a shell with two halves (also called valves) and a soft body. Snails, slugs, and conches are known as gastropods. Most gastropods have a shell, although some do not. They also have a muscular foot, and many have a ring of teeth called a radula. About 65 percent of mollusks belong to this class.

Octopuses, squid, cuttlefish, and nautiluses are in a group called

This diagram shows mollusks from several classes.

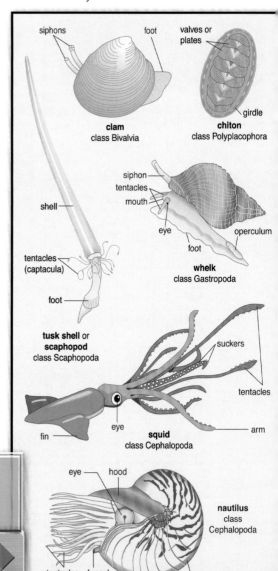

Chitons are an unusual kind of mollusk. They have eight separate valves!

COMPARE AND CONTRAST

Compare and contrast the bivalves, gastropods, and cephalopods. How are they similar? How are they different?

cephalopods. Cephalopods swim and generally do not have shells. They have the most developed brain and eyes of all mollusks. The biggest mollusks belong to this class.

BIVALVES

Bivalves have a shell with two halves, or valves. There are about 15,000 species of bivalves. Clams, oysters, mussels, and scallops are some of the most commonly known. Most bivalves live in the ocean, but a few species live in fresh water. They can be tiny or very large. Giant clams can weigh more than 500 pounds (227 kilograms)!

Bivalves have a nervous system, a digestive system, and a heart. They have gills instead of lungs. A hard shell protects the soft body. Muscles connect the two halves of the shell, which allow it to

Two hard shells are protecting this scallop's soft body.

THINK ABOUT IT

Consider the parts of a bivalve's body. How does each part help it to survive?

There are many species of clams, including quahogs (*left*) and soft-shelled clams (*right*).

close quickly and tightly. The shell opens when these muscles relax.

Bivalve species behave in different ways. Oysters and ocean mussels attach themselves to solid surfaces. Scallops swim by clapping the halves of their shell together. Clams and freshwater mussels dig into the sand with their muscular foot.

GASTROPODS

THINK ABOUT IT

Snails and slugs are some of the only land-dwelling mollusks. How are these gastropods adapted to life on land?

Gastropods are the largest group of mollusks. The group contains more than 65,000 species! They include snails, slugs, and sea slugs. Most gastropods have one shell. The shells are commonly coiled and can have beautiful colors and patterns. Slugs—both on land and in the sea—do not have a shell.

Gastropods have a head and a soft body. They have a complete digestive system and highly

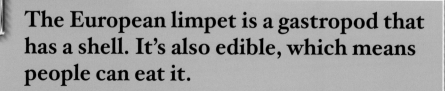

The European limpet is a gastropod that has a shell. It's also edible, which means people can eat it.

developed sense organs. On land, snails and slugs release slime from their body, which they glide over as they move.

Gastropods are found throughout the world. Some land gastropods spend the winter underground. Gastropods feed using a structure called the radula. The radula is covered with rows of tiny teeth. Gastropods use the tiny teeth for grinding food and scraping it off surfaces.

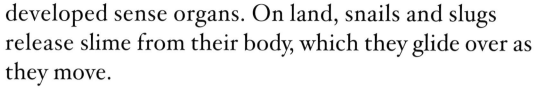

The brown garden snail is a gastropod commonly found in gardens.

CEPHALOPODS

Cephalopods look nothing like most other mollusks. There are 650 species of cephalopods. The group includes octopuses, squid, nautiluses, and cuttlefish. These mollusks are active predators, feeding on fish and crustaceans.

Cephalopods are very smart creatures. They have a big head, which contains a large brain. They also have a complex nervous system and highly developed eyes. Cephalopods commonly have eight to

The chambered nautilus is the only cephalopod that has a fully developed shell.

COMPARE AND CONTRAST

Look at a picture of an octopus, squid, nautilus, and cuttlefish. What do they have in common? How are they different?

ten tentacles. The tentacles are covered with suckers, which help the cephalopod catch prey or attach to hard surfaces.

Generally, cephalopods do not have a shell. Instead, they protect themselves by swimming and moving quickly. Squid and octopuses can change color and patterns to blend into their surroundings. Most can also squirt an inky substance when an enemy is near. It makes the water cloudy—a perfect distraction while the cephalopod escapes!

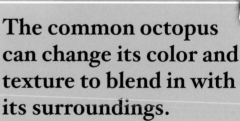

The common octopus can change its color and texture to blend in with its surroundings.

WHERE MOLLUSKS LIVE

Mollusks can be found throughout the world. Most live in oceans, which are salty, but others live in fresh water. Some mollusks like shallow water along the coast. Others prefer deep water—some have been found at depths of 2,200 feet (670 meters)! Many mollusks dig into sandy or muddy bottoms, but some attach

Many mollusks live along coastlines.

themselves to rocks. Oysters, for example, grow in huge stacks called clusters. The majority of mollusks are free-living species, which means they do not have a permanent home. Some mollusk species are parasites and live on or inside another living thing.

Mollusks also live on land, even in our backyards! A garden is a perfect home for snails and slugs. These terrestrial mollusks generally like cool, moist places. However, they are also found in cold regions and in dry deserts.

Vocabulary

Terrestrial means living on or in land, or growing from land.

Gastropods are a common sight in gardens. Be careful, or else they'll eat your plants!

MOLLUSKS IN ECOSYSTEMS

Land-bound mollusks play a big part in keeping this soil healthy.

An ecosystem is a community of living creatures that rely on each other for survival. Mollusks are an important part of their ecosystem. Terrestrial gastropods like snails and slugs put nutrients back into the soil as they eat. This keeps their habitat healthy.

Bivalves are also an important part of their ecosystem. They play a big part in cleaning Earth's waters by filtering sediments out of the water as they eat. One adult oyster can filter about 50 gallons (190 liters) of water a day! This makes the water clean and clear—a healthy home for other marine creatures.

Cephalopods are important to their ecosystem because they are predators. They feed on fish, crabs, lobsters, and other marine animals, which keeps the ecosystem balanced. When an ecosystem is balanced, every species can survive.

THINK ABOUT IT

All organisms in an ecosystem share their habitat's resources, including food and living space. Why is balance important in an ecosystem?

Earth's water ecosystems wouldn't be healthy without mollusks.

Life Cycle of a Mollusk

Bivalves begin life as a fertilized egg. In most marine bivalves, the egg hatches into a larva. Larvae are wormlike creatures that look very different from the adult animal. Most bivalves actually have two larval stages. During these stages, the larvae are free swimming. After some time, the larvae fall to the sea floor and attach to a hard surface. When they become adults, they no longer swim.

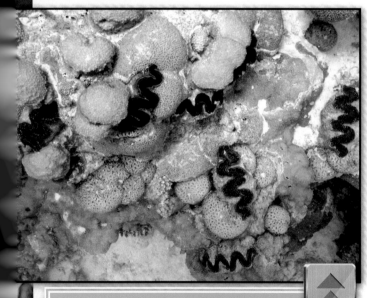

These giant clams are attached to a coral reef.

COMPARE AND CONTRAST

Compare and contrast the life cycle of the three major mollusk classes.

Gastropods begin life in a similar way to bivalves. The fertilized egg hatches into a free-swimming larva. During the larval stage, the gastropod's body twists to bring the lower half of the body to the top. This is called torsion and only occurs in gastropods. They then grow into adults.

Female cephalopods lay clusters of eggs on the ocean floor, under rocks, or on hard surfaces. Some females protect the eggs until they hatch. After hatching, the young look like small adults, or they may go through a larval stage.

These snail eggs will hatch into tiny snails one day.

FEEDING HABITS

What does a mollusk eat for dinner? Many mollusks eat mostly algae. Gastropods use their radula to scrape algae off rocks. Larger mollusks have a bigger appetite. Snails and slugs eat plants and fruit. Squid may eat fish and shrimp. An octopus can go after prey as large as a shark!

Bivalves are filter feeders. That means they eat by straining tiny particles of food from the water. When

THINK ABOUT IT

How are mollusks' bodies adapted to help them hunt or feed?

The algae covering this rock make a tasty meal for gastropods.

bivalves open their shell, water washes over the gills. The gills then strain out oxygen and food.

Mollusks usually are active at night. Octopuses stay in the deep ocean during the day. At dawn and dusk, they swim closer to the surface looking for food. Giant squid use their foot-wide eye to see prey in the dark ocean. Terrestrial snails and slugs hide during the day and come out at night.

anterior adductor muscle
digestive gland
stomach
aorta
esophagus
heart
mouth
kidney
shell
posterior adductor muscle
anus
foot
excurrent siphon
ganglion
intestine
incurrent siphon
mantle
gills

© 2014 Merriam-Webster, Inc.

This is what the inside of a clam looks like. Water will pass through its shell and over its soft body.

Humans and Mollusks

Mollusks have been important to humans for a long time. Many mollusks are a source of food for people around the world. Clams, oysters, scallops, octopus, and squid are the most commonly eaten mollusks. In France, *escargots*—or snails—are a delicacy.

Gathering and selling mollusks are important to the economy of many places along seacoasts. Mother-of-pearl, a shiny material

One type of mollusk is the star ingredient in this popular dish— clam chowder!

on bivalve shells, is used for buttons and decorations. People use mollusk shells to make jewelry and other objects. Certain species of oysters make beautiful pearls, a valuable gemstone. And if you've ever collected seashells on the beach, you are likely holding part of a mollusk.

THINK ABOUT IT

Humans have used mollusks for food and as part of their economy for thousands of years. What could happen if mollusk populations decline?

Some oysters produce pearls inside their shells. The pearls form around small bits of sand or grit.

MOLLUSKS AT RISK

Mollusks have been on the planet for millions of years. In fact, some mollusk species are among the oldest-known animals. Mollusks have survived because their bodies are very well-adapted to their environment. However, Earth's climate is changing, and the changes are affecting mollusks.

Global warming is causing the air temperatures on Earth to rise. As the planet warms, water

This fossil is of a snail that lived millions of years ago.

VOCABULARY

Global warming is the observable increase of the surface temperature on Earth. When people burn coal, oil, and other fossil fuels, certain gases are released into the atmosphere. These gases trap energy from the sun and warm the atmosphere.

temperatures also rise. Mollusks that thrive in cool temperatures are struggling to survive in warmer waters because their bodies are not adapted to the warmer temperatures.

Human behavior is responsible for other problems that are having a negative effect on mollusk habitats as well. For example, overfishing and pollution are causing mollusk populations to decline.

Large fishing boats are a threat to mollusks. If they catch too many, mollusks could die out.

Making a Mollusk-Friendly World

It is important to think about how our actions affect

mollusks. Mollusks are an important source of food and have played a big role in the economy of places along seacoasts. We also need mollusks to keep Earth's ecosystems

Coastlines are for people to enjoy, but we must keep them safe for mollusks, too.

THINK ABOUT IT
What are some ways you can make the world a better place for mollusks?

balanced. We depend on mollusks in important ways, so it is important that we respect them.

You are never too young to help make the planet a better place for mollusks. One of the best ways to help is to think about the impact you have on the environment. Talk to your teacher and family about ways you can keep our planet safe and clean for mollusks and all living organisms. When the world is safe for mollusks, it helps us, too.

This man is cleaning up an oil spill in a body of water in Kansas.

Glossary

adapt To change in order to fit a new situation.

characteristic A quality or appearance that makes an individual or group different from others.

climate The average weather conditions of a particular place or region over a period of years.

cluster A number of similar things growing, collected, or grouped together.

digestive system The parts of the body that work together to change food into a form that the body can use.

diverse Differing from one another.

muscle A body tissue consisting of long cells that can contract to produce motion.

nervous system The organ system that carries messages from the brain to other parts of the body.

nutrient Tiny substances in food that living things eat, drink, or absorb to grow and survive.

organ A part of the body that consists of cells and tissues and is specialized to do a particular task.

pollution The action or process of making land, water, or air dirty and not safe or suitable to use.

prey An animal that is hunted or killed by another animal for food.

resource Something that is found in nature and helps living things survive.

varied Having many forms or types.

FOR MORE INFORMATION

Books

Bishop, Celeste. *Slimy Slugs*. New York, NY: PowerKids Press, 2016.

Boothroyd, Jennifer. *Shells*. Minneapolis, MN: Lerner, 2012.

Housel, Debra J. *Incredible Invertebrates*. Huntington Beach, CA: Teacher Created Materials, 2012.

Montgomery, Sy and Keith A. Ellenbogen. *The Octopus Scientists: Exploring the Mind of a Mollusk*. Boston, MA: Houghton Mifflin Harcourt, 2015.

Murphy, Emily. *Bay in the Balance*. Monterey, CA: National Geographic, 2013.

Petersen, Christine. *Pearls*. Minneapolis, MN: ABDO Publishing Company, 2014.

Websites

Because of the changing nature of internet links, Rosen Publishing has developed an online list of websites related to the subject of this book. This site is updated regularly. Please use this link to access this list:

http://www.rosenlinks.com/LFO/moll

INDEX